ıe Fall of the Angels, A Sacred Poem by John William Polidori

n William Polidori was born on 7th September 1795 in London to Gaetano Polidori, an Italian political igré scholar, and Anna Maria Pierce, an English governess. He was the eldest of 8 children.

m 1804 Polidori was a pupil at the recently formed Ampleforth College. In 1810 he proceeded to the versity of Edinburgh, where he wrote a thesis on sleepwalking and received his degree as a doctor of dicine on 1st August 1815. He was 19.

.816, Dr. Polidori was given the job of Byron's personal physician and accompanied him on a trip ough Europe. The publisher John Murray offered Polidori £500 to keep a diary of their travels. At the a Diodati, Byron's rented villa at Lake Geneva in Switzerland, the pair met with Mary Wollstonecraft dwin, Percy Bysshe Shelley, and Mary's stepsister, Claire Clairmont.

e night in June, after the company had read aloud from a French collection of German horror tales, on suggested they each write a ghost story. There were to be two outstanding works from that ning; 'Frankenstein' by Mary Shelley and Polidori's 'The Vampyre' which would be the first published dern vampire story in English.

missed by Byron, Polidori traveled in Italy and then returned to England. His story, 'The Vampyre', s published in the April 1819 issue of New Monthly Magazine without his permission. Much to the oyance of both Polidori and Byron it was the latter who was credited as author.

idori also had published 'Ximenes, The Wreath & Other Poems' in 1819 and his long theological and red poem 'The Fall of the Angels' in 1821 as well as two plays, essays and his diary.

spite his youth Polidori was increasingly worn down by gambling debts and depression.

n William Polidori died on 24th August 1821 at the age of only 25 in London. Although his death was orded as death by natural causes, strong evidence asserts that it was suicide by means of cyanide.

dex of Contents

E FALL OF THE ANGELS

NTO THE FIRST

E ARGUMENT

The Creation of the World, I. Chaos. **III.** The alarm of the newly created angel's at hearing the nds of such confusion. **IV.** Their flight to the Godhead. **V.** His pity wakens Mercy, who destroys the confusion. **VI.** A description of the rising worlds. **VIII.** The angels hasten to gaze upon them. **X.** The creation of vegetation and animals.

§ 2. The Creation of the Human Form. XI. No one can tell where God resides in splendour. **XII.** The angels cannot look upon him. **XIII.** The angels pray to partake in the active love that inspires the whole of God's works. **XVII.** They remain prostrate at his feet, while Nature is alarmed at their daring. **XIX.** U God answers, and forms a human body, when she is reassured and exults.

§ 3. The Fall of the Angels, XXI. A description of man's form. **XXIII.** Jehovah calls upon the yet prostrat angels to rear their heads and view his late creation. Their surprise and astonishment. **XXIV.** Some ado God and return to him. **XXV.** One of those yet remaining near the body addresses the others, and laughing at the weakness of the being they are to serve, excites to rebellion. **XXVII.** The indignation of heaven and earth. **XXIX.** A battle between the good and bad angels, the latter are overcome and brought before God.

§ 4, The Animation of Man. XXXI. God's sentence on the fallen angels. The instigator's spirit is the first that begins its suffering: it animates the body of Adam. **XXXII.** The angels hasten round the animated form of man to guard it, the demons to tempt it. **XXXIII.** The effect of day. **XXXIV.** Of night upon him. **XXXVI.** He feels the want of a voice, and the power of communication with the objects round. **XXXVII.** He finds a voice. **XXXVIII.** He finds himself a solitary being in the vast world, in which nothing sympathizes with him. His complaint.

§ 5. The Creation of Woman, and the Fall of Man. XL. The creation of woman. **XLI.** Power of beauty counteracted by the influence of evil. **XLIV.** Adam tired of love, begins to feel the desire of knowledge, and deserts Eve. **XLV.** Eve wanders about disconsolate, meets with the tree of knowledge. **XLVIII.** The devil, in the disguise of a serpent, tempts her to eat. She eats. **XLIX.** The devil's apostrophe to God, an Adam's vision of mankind's future fate.

TO THE DEITY

A storm may gather fore the orb of day
And seem to threaten ruin to the plain;
The sun sends hope upon a golden ray
To write upon its edge "I'll shine again."
The night striding towards the reddening west
Steps to the earth and spreads her hideous vest;

Beneath its weight man pauses in his will,
And crouches at the dark-robed phantom's feet:
But soon the veil is raised; the russet hill
Begins to smile, the song of birds to greet
The nymph, who, running fore the weary wain.
Cries from the mountains top "He'll shine again."

So on grief's thick'ning clouds, despair's fell night, there breaks
God's promise, and our soul secure and smiling wakes.

THE FALL OF THE ANGELS

CANTO THE FIRST.

SECTION I.

THE CREATION OF THE WORLD.

I.

Through infinite, eternal space 'twas night
And darkness: scarcely the blue lightning shone.
As, flashing idly thro' its harmless flight,
It lit discordant elements alone.
Oblivion spread its vast long limbs, with sullen pride.
Midst the loved, changeless shades, that everything could hide;
No speck of beauty, sparkling there on high.
As some meek flower, that breaks the snow to shine,
No sun sail'd, like a ship, across the sky,
A startling show of pomp and power divine.

II.

Then sounds alone, like Etna's breathings, broke
Upon the wilder'd ear of Seraphim,
And seem'd as if the presence they bespoke
Of one who mock'd at God and scoff'd at him.
For element 'gainst element was loudly warring.
And latent flames, and waves, and rocks, were broken jarring;
Then were unknown fair music's magic power.
The still soft sounding of the speaking wave.
The rolling erash of clouds, that proudly lower
As if the Almighty used the voice they gave.

III.

Soon as created. Angels trembling stood,
To hear the chaos loud, with 'palling sound
Of stormy elements a mingling flood,
Strike 'gainst its shore, and strike but to rebound;
Its huge waves, rushing, met the presence of a God,
And weakening strove in vain, where'er his footsteps trod:
Seraphs, Dominions, Powers created rose.
Then fled, impetuous, to their maker's breast;

Trembling they crouch'd, and wilder'd fancied foes
Would lift from out the huge abyss their crest.

IV.

Bending and mute, with agitated eye,
And trembling limbs, and pallid cheeks and lips.
The Angels tow'rds the Godhead troubled fly,
As fore the raging storm men's crowding ships.
Hastening around their God, haggard they clung, they prest;
Alone, beaming serene, upon his face, were signs of rest.
Thus can the shepherd, when the forest near
Echoes the howling wolf's loud lengthening bay.
Sleep undismayed, the while his sheep, with fear,
Wilder'd look round and know not where to stay.

V.

He saw their fear. Reclined beneath his throne.
Wrapt in his garments, sleeping Mercy wakes;
She moves, and sound is still, confusion gone;
Whilst heavenly music, soft, slow, stealing breaks
Upon the doubting sense of reassured crowds.
From spheres that, rolling now, no darkness shrouds.
God will'd, and space, though infinite, was still;
A thousand, then ten thousand orbs appear'd
Rolling in light, obedient to his will;
His will they sought, his guiding breath revered

VI.

Faint type, the sun, that sudden splendent breaks
The canopy of black beleaguer'd clouds,
That darken o'er the earth: while Vengeance wreaks
The human wrongs of him whom nature shrouds;
While shaking mountains fear the flashing thunder's hate,
And Nature fainting seems to sink beneath her fate.
Sudden its beam, at once, may give to sight
The wave that sparkles in the sailor's way.
The glittering foliage nodding in its light,
The smiling rock that reddens in its ray.

VII.

Still what are these? They are but earthly show!
To Angels then vast infinite was one!
And can aught bright compare of here below
With these young orbs, all dancing round their sun
And slowly rising into space, that knew not time,
As summer's golden orb unto a Lapland clime?
With that bright show, not e'en that East compares,
When glorious, calling man from fear and rest,
The sun rouses the russet dawn, and tears
The wintry veil from Nature's snowy breast.

VIII.

Caught by the sound, attracted by the scene
That breaks upon his sense with virgin light,
As if a hand had drawn the hiding screen
And shown all nature to his wilder'd sight,
A Cherub spreads his wings, a moment doubting stands,
Then sudden laughs and springs and flutters o'er new lands;
Then thronging Angels his bright track pursue.
As birds, whose leader o'er the Asiatic plain,
Where torrents spread their waters to the view,
In varying line conducts a noisy train.

IX.

Then seem'd each Seraph but a sportive child.
To whom her mother shows the robe of spring;
By flowers, sparkling with dew, she runs beguiled,
And hope and pleasure seem her feet to wing;
Charm'd by the various hue, at last, she doubtful stands
And feasts her eager eyes forgetful of her hands.
Thus sped each Seraph o'er the shining fields.
Lured by the orbs that move in splendid strife;
Unknowing which to which in beauty yields.
Hovering, they wake new worlds to sounds of life.

X.

Yet all was barren; nothing but a stream
Of splendent suns and stars attracts the sight:
Mingling, they deckt each other with a gleam,
Each caught its beauty from its brother's light.
But, by the grateful sight of seraphs' joy beguiled,
Jehovah, pleased, look'd on his vast work and smiled

Then suddenly they see the planets move.
They see, upon the barren glittering earth.
The bending corn, the forests, nodding grove.
And worlds and oceans teeming one great birth..

SECTION II.

THE CREATION OF THE HUMAN FORM.

XI.

What tongue shall say where the Almighty's throned?
Where, in his silent majesty and power,
He wields the sceptre, with no jewels stoned.
But with a sun, that forms the summit's flower?
Where, brilliant with his crown of various sparkling star,
His head, rear'd into space, looks down upon the Car?
An eagle's eye may gaze on founts of light,
A mole's may pierce the earth's obscurity;
No mortal eye has gain'd the dazzling sight
Of great Jehovah in his purity

XII.

Hardly the Angels gaze upon his brow,
When, falling prostrate 'neath his footstool's shade,
They pray that he should veil the awful show
Of splendent power, that causes sight to fade.
lie gathers murky shades of thickest darkness round.
And crowding mists, to form the Godhead's veil, are found;
But, as the sun, e'en thro' the gathering cloud,
That lifts its fleecy mass on some huge rock,
Pierces the envious, the life-hiding shroud,
So majesty its thickening veil doth mock.

XIII.

No Angel raised his humble bending head;
But one great voice burst from each beating breast:
Not such the thunders, when the storm is led.
Midst echoing rocks,- from the high mountain's crest.
It fill'd the firmament, and, borne upon the breeze
Of thousand planets, echoed o'er their splashing seas.
At once the voice of birds join'd in the sound,

Learning the song, with which they, after night.
Have since call'd Nature, in sleep's thraldom bound.
To wake and view God's purest emblem light.

XIV.

"O Power! known but by works, that show thy will
Omnipotent, we have pursued thy breath,
Amidst the spheres, which e'en vast space can fill
With gems, that form unto each sun a wreath,
Thy beams, too powerful for Angels' weaker sight,
Sent from thy gladdening brow, afford the suns their light.
The suns bestow upon each circling earth
A portion of their pride, reflecting rays.
From which these orbs give forth one various birth.
And life springs forth and decks fair heaven's ways.

XV.

"The huge behemoth, troubling all the sea,
The ant, that treads the moveless grain of sand,
The mountain, snatching from the clouds, that flee
Across the heaven, the weapons of their hand.
Seek not their good alone; but all thy wondrous works
Shield or protect each other, whene'er danger lurks.
They all within their narrow sphere can show
The hand of Him that gave them living force;
Within the very rocks there seems to glow
Reflection of some beam, from their first source

XVI.

"We, we alone first creatures of thy will,
More deckt with strength and power and various grace,
Seem but to live for self; but self mayn't fill
The heart, wherein thy kindling power we trace.
Thy touch is love, and mercy dwells within thy breast,
Tempering the will, that waked the world from fitful rest,
O sovereign Power! but will that we obtain
Our share in acting what thy nature loves;
Then happiness will be thy servants' gain.
Whene'er thy smile our humbler work approves."

XVII.

As lilies that for days have drooping hung,
Scorch'd up, await the clouds, that bid them pine,
So these ne'er raised their heads, but having sung.
Yet prostrate lay and wait the word divine.
Within their breasts was hope; but fear and anxious doubt
Strode, dancing, round their hearts, mingling their sickening
When, sudden as the child who fears the voice shouts:
Of its kind mother, if some fault is done.
Let her but smile, e'en quickly can rejoice.
So Angels woke to joy; their hopes are won.

XVIII.

A voice, as of ten thousand organs, rose
Swelling from the soft note to the loud sound
That rivals thunder, when the anthems close
With notes that, struck from the groin'd roof, rebound.
The mists went rolling from the face of sovereign power,
Driven by his breath, they broke, and veil'd the God no more;
Beneath his feet, the new-born fabric shook.
And chaos beat against high heaven's walls;
As lashing wave, whene'er a bank is broke,
Exulting at the thought of foe that falls.

XIX.

The Godhead spoke, and all his works were still.
As the poor shipwreck, on a lonely rock,
Round which the ocean steals, knows fear and chill,
Whene'er the raging waves break with loud shock;
But if at length a ship in the far mist he spies.
He joys, and o'er the seas are echoed his wild cries;
So Nature felt, chaotic Ocean raged.
And round her form his misshaped arms he threw;
The voice assured her, and, her fears assuaged,
She joy'd, while backwards trembling Chaos flew

XX.

"Angels! you shall have beings to protect;
But know, that, where the power of ill is given,
If good come thence, e'en thrones you must erect,
And you from lofty primacy are driven;
For virtue, higher than all power, mocks at the show

That strength may seem to give, or pomp or aught bestow."
He said, and to the earth he, stooping, took
Clay from the river's bed, and form'd a man
Wanting a soul, although the form partook
Of majesty like that which Angels scan.

SECTION III.

THE FALL OF THE ANGELS.

XXI.

The form, created, lay upon a bank
Gemm'd with the fragrant flowers of infant spring,
Shelter'd by trees, whose leaves from fountains drank
That slowly murmur'd stillness whispering.
Upon his brow it seem'd that majesty asleep,
Upon his lips that graces hung in slumbers deep.
The dark long hair upon the tranquil breast;
The pencil'd eyelash, breaking with its line
The quiet cheek, where roses seem'd to rest;
The limbs seem'd all with innocence to shine.

XXII.

When virtue's struggle ends, and taunts are vain;
When all the world's inflictions can no more;
When virtue gains a refuge from all pain,
And pure has run its course on this wild shore;
When stormy manhood sinks, as infancy was born,
With smiles of peace, unstain'd, tho' e'en by passion torn;
Then even death may wear that pleasing look
This form then bore, when, fresh from God's fair hand,
That smile, as if the dead of rest, partook
Without a triumph o'er th' oppressive band.

XXIII.

Jehovah spoke, and bade the bending choirs
Now raise their heads and view the form of man,
That form, which animate to heaven aspires
And seeks eternity and God to scan;
That form, which by its act may gain the lofty seat,
Where virtue is secure reward and joys to meet.

They stood erect and eager look'd around;
They gazed below, thinking midst stars to see
Some being fluttering o'er the azure ground,
Deckt in the gayest glittering panoply;

XXIV.

Then turn'd their eyes upon the ocean's space,
Thinking some form might meet their anxious sight,
Playing with its oft deeply dimpled face,
Or struggling with its waves in equal fight;
Then on the Alps, the lofty Andes, fixt they gazed,
Thinking he play'd with lightnings that their summit grazed.
But, when, stretcht out, they saw the weakly frame.
Wondering they view'd, e'en by amazement won;
Then, bowing meekly, thousands backwards came.
And at God's throne sung out "Thy will be done."

XXV.

But one, midst others, radiant with gold scales.
That cover'd all his frame, brilliant to sight,
With two huge wings, that flap the perfumed gales,
Bearing such hues as pass'd the iris'd light.
Hovering, at length stood sudden on the loaded earth,
And, laughing, thus address'd the crowd with cheating mirth:
"Is this the form that we must serve and guide?
Must we forget the paths of brilliant skies.
And stand for ever by this mortal's side.
While he to gain our seats, our birthright tries?

XXVI.

"Who has e'er seen the lordly lion care
The reptile shaking at his awful brow?
Who has e'er seen the lofty oak to share
The trembling fears the reed alone may know?
Shall we, whose flight can reach the presence of a God,
Shall we depend on such a feeble worldling's nod?"
E'en as he spoke, loud murmurings arose,
And whisperings of discontent and spite;
As each to each his grief, his trouble shows,
Gradually shouts rise to heaven's height.

XXVII.

The sound, circling the throne, threw wild dismay
And horror to the breasts of bending choirs.
The thunders broke from where they sleeping lay;
The angry lightnings flash'd with forked fires;
The clouds, the footstool, and the throne, indignant shook,
While God into his hand his golden balance took.
Trembling, the Angels hid beneath their wings
Their quailing brows, and only lowly cried
"Mercy!" The beam the scale of mercy flings
High to the heavens, and their cause is tried.

XXVIII.

The earth shook trembling from the East to West;
The giant ocean lash'd its bounds with ire;
The clouds Hew rapid from the azure breast
And show'd the offending children to their sire.
God will'd: with anxious haste the myriads instant fly
To bring their brothers fore the insulted deity.
la vain they plead the Godhead's mercies shown,
In vain they plead the sinner's hope secure:
When once the soul the thorn of vice has known,
Nought but its bitter fruits the wound can cure.

XXIX.

A mighty struggle and a fight arose;
War now disturbs the earth's unbroken rest;
A mighty river waves and foam oft throws
Against a rock, rebounding from its breast;
So, for a time, the Angels' dreadful strife was vain;
No one could o'er the other any vantage gain.
Their huge spread limbs in dreadful contact came
And struggling fell, enclasp'd, upon the ground;
The mountains shook, beams of the world's vast frame,
They seem'd to sink and creaking yield around.

XXX.

Their shouts, their cries of triumph and of pain
Mock'd Etna's throes, when, heaving all its mass,
It frights mankind. Their blood, one bright vast stain
Spreads o'er the mead and reddens all the grass.

But what is strength, against that smile the heavens bestow
On those within whose breast is known great virtue's glow?
Arm'd by such spell, the weak can shame the strong,
The simple fool can baffle e'en the sage:
These ministers of God ne'er battled long,
But chain'd the foes who battle dared to wage.

SECTION IV.

THE ANIMATION OF MAN.

XXXI.

To leave the forms on which they placed their pride,
To seek the human frame they scoff'd at now,
And there, unknowing of the past reside,
Living and dying, while long ages flow.
Until, tho' knowing evil, good should he obtain'd;
Such was the milder sentence God for these ordain'd.
And lifeless, first, the beauteous spoil is seen
Of him who urged them rashly to the deed;
While man's arose from off the flowery green,
Fired with a soul that mock'd such idle weed.

XXXII.

The Angels gazed, then sang the mercied word
That gave their brothers hope of future rest,
And hastening fly and anxiously afford
Their guardian power, gainst man's tumultuous breast.
Showing the love that sway'd th' omnipotence divine,
They hoped, at once, to place man in his now lost shrine.
The demons too, for such they now became,
Tainted by evil and rebellious guilt,
Round the light form in thickening numbers came,
And strove to break the hopes the Angels built.

XXXIII.

Man rose: his dark black eye gleam'd from its nest,
And seem'd, with thirst, to drink the glorious sight;
Wonder and awe went revelling in his breast;
He seem'd as drunk with such excess of light.
He moved, and from the shade of trees burst on his eyes

That orb, fore whom e'en fear with night for ever flies.
He look'd, till his sight fail'd, then strove to hide,
With his soft hands, the vision from his gaze;
But still it seem'd as if the streaming tide
Of beams burst thro' the veil by unknown ways.

XXXIV.

At last again he look'd; the waving trees,
The thronging flowers sprinkled o'er the earth,
The blossoms wanton on the playful breeze,
Forming a bath of odour round his birth.
The sparkling waters gilt like moving waves of gold.
The azure sky, fore which the clouds their crimson hold.
All caught, in turns, his now bewilder'd mind;
He watch'd the sun sink glorious in the west;
Then turn'd himself, and was amazed to find
That o'er tlie whole was drawn a darkening vest.

XXXV.

E'en like a child, he grieved to lose the show
Of gaudy colours glittering on the sky.
Of light, gay sparkling on the waters flow;
He fear'd it was a dream, that thus could fly.
He laid him down, fatigued he sunk to peaceful sleep,
And there imagined his, what erst he could not keep.
The moon was pausing midway, taking rest,
When, wakening into sense, he felt the peace
That night can breathe upon the human breast
With the mild ray of its light starry fleece.

XXXVI.

Till now his bosom, bustling with its thought,
View'd nature only as a splendid show,
That might reward the eye whose glance it caught;
But gave not to the soul aught else to know.
Now, that nocturnal stillness silenced all the sound
Of nature, save the voice which can within resound.
He felt a struggling, which oppres'd his heart
With sickening eagerness, that e'en seem'd vain,
From thought and all that press'd on thought to part,
And some communion with the world to gain.

XXXVII.

All was yet still, the stream murmur'd alone.
And spoke of time, while silence touch'd the earth
When on the path of day, by morning shown,
The sun came riding in his car of mirth.
And as he paced, he changed the dew-beweeping sky
Into a bride treading on gems of revelry.
Adam fell down, and form'd at last a voice
That bursting said "Thy power indeed is great."
Hardly he spoke, when all with him rejoice,
The breezes, birds, all that has tongue to greet.

XXXVIII.

Lured by the sounds that from the woodlands seem,
He trod the wood's bewildering winding ways,
Caught on the fanning breeze a pleasing dream,
Of nature answering, with affection's lays.
To his heart's craving, and his speech with hers did float,
Until he found she always answer'd the same note.
Until he saw that every beast with haste
Flew from his steps, and own'd no other mate
Than one on whom its lineaments were traced:
Then he bewail'd his miserable fate.

XXXIX.

"Am I alone, like yonder orb of speed,
To run round this wide world, a grieving form
Unmatcht, unfriended, while no one shall heed,
Lost in their joys, my soul's afflicting storm?
The lion and the emmet, and the wandering breeze
Find all a fondling mate, whom with their love they please;
But my hoarse voice finds but the echo's tone,
That gives me sounds; it speaks my words again,
But answers not, and I am still alone,"
E'en such until he slept his mournful strain.

SECTION V.

THE CREATION OF WOMAN, AND THE FALL OF MAN.

XL.

But what is that which stands before his sight,
A wakening dream of beauty and of joy?
Aroused he rises, wilder'd with delight,
One object seems his every thought t' employ.
Heaven's gift, a lovely woman, stands before his feet,
And with entrancing presence makes his sorrows fleet.
She seems, and is, sufficient to outweigh
E'en hell's inflictions; Iris to his heart,
She 'twixt despair and heaven reflects a ray
Of God, and seems his presence to impart.

XLI.

There is a power in beauty, that will bless;
Tho' man resist, when woman's sunlike smile
Breaks on his passions, he is bitterless.
And seems, at once, unconscious of all guile.
The peasant muttering looks upon the battling clouds,
But cheers, whene'er the sun his joyful brow unshrouds;
And man, sickening with pain, by anguish driven.
Looking regretful on the hopes he rear'd.
Which suddenly by despair's fell touch are riven,
Raises his head and laughs by woman chear'd.

XLII.

Her sparkling eye sends forth such dazzling light,
He deems it sprung from those encircling beams
That deck some being, with high splendour bright.
Who sends us hope, on these reflected gleams,
To say, he soon, in all his radiant brilliance deckt.
Will forth and realize what fancy dreams uncheckt.
When God gave woman to man's restless heart.
It seem'd as if such gift, at once, should chain
And e'en to virtue bind him ne'er to part;
But not, for her, can he from guilt refrain.

XLIII.

For evil has such power, that e'en with Man,
Heaven's brightest gift but tempts the more his will
To crowd with every wrong his short-lived span,
Until perchance his death the measure fill.

E'en now to Man was given a smile-creating bride.
Who placed on him her love and in his joy her pride,
Whose tender limbs, that seem for weakness framed.
Shun no fatigue, but oftener shun repose.
In search of what man's wantonness has claim'd,
Until e'en blood doth stain her brighter snows.

XLIV.

Now, tired at length of fondling and of love.
He looks upon the sun, and wishes glow
That he might guide the car its spirit drove,
And view what earth can give to sight below.
He climb'd the moantain's top, and sought the giant hand
That threw its lightnings thence upon the quailing land.
He sought in the dark cavern's murky depth.
Passing the beams that bear the world's mass'd wall,
The demon raising the sick earth with breath
That dims all heaven and makes nature pall.

XLV.

While Eve went mourning o'er her widow'd heart,
Wandering o'er hill and far far spreading wood,
She call'd on him, who would ere morn depart
And not regard her charms, her sorrow's flood.
Mourning she went, unconscious of the lengthening way.
Until she saw a tree all sparkling in the day.
Its bright green leaves e'en half reveal'd half hid
Fair fruits, that seem'd to blush and seek the shade.
As virgin does, who in great haste has bid
Her veil to fall, which, lingering, has betrayed.

XLVI.

It was the Tree of knowledge and of life,
Which they, forbid'n to taste, had ne'er approach'd;
The fruitful dew, that touch'd its leaves, fell rife,
And plants sprung up and on its boughs encroach'd.
Breathless, alarm'd that her unconscious steps had trod
So near the spot where stood what was forbid'n by God,
She was about to turn; when from the tree
A voice came forth, with sounds so soft and sweet,
That she entranced stood still: from terror free.
She felt a hope some blessing sprite to meet.

XLVII.

The leaves are rustling, and at last appears
A form glittering with scales of thousand lights;
Slowly its pointed head it lofty rears,
And thus with words deceives, with hope delights:
"Mother of a race that on the future throws
A spell, and power o'er all thro' which life eddying flows!
O first alike in beauty and in race!
God's proudest work, decking the flowery earth
With what e'en heaven might adorn and grace!
Fairest enchantress! creature of light mirth!

XLVIII.

"Why should you sigh and grieve alone below?
Is it because your lover stays away.
And seeks to pierce the hidden cause's flow?
Then change at once your darkness into day.
This fruit, that seems, denying, half to woo the sight,
At once lifts up the veil that shuts his eyes from light.
That you might show your love unto your mate.
By daring ill to fall upon your head.
Made God forbid this tree; on you now wait
Your husband's hopes; they soon for e'er are fled."

XLIX.

The demon, lurking in the serpent's coil,
Spoke cheating thus; and Eve, with hurried pace,
Rush'd to the tree and fell within his toil.
Then flash'd his eye with pride, with joy his face.
"Now may the wondrous God, who boasts his sovereign power,
Own me his foe; nor let his brow contemptuous lower,
If I too boast, who've mock'd his kind intent
Of making us in human forms reside.
And there do penance and in tears repent,
For what we did when sitting by his side."

L.

The serpent's hollow coil fell lifeless down. —
On Adam and on Eve's mind sickening burst

The certainty of toil and sickness, shown
In a dead vision, where they seemed curst.
And where Envy, Revenge and Malice sporting danced
Around a bloody form, that seem'd in thought entranced.
While, looking upon weapons black with gore.
Its silent finger beckon'd Love and Hate
To come and take; from the red muddy floor
A dagger to fulfill the bitter fate.

CANTO THE SECOND.

THE ARGUMENT.

§ 1. The Deluge. II. Man's increasing; guilt; he insults the Deity with mocking words. **III.** Vengeance cleaves the rocks, and opens the abyss beneath the earth. The firmament is broken, and its reservoirs are poured upon the earth. **IV.** The screams and shrieks of men. The crowded mass of a town is forced to leave the wreck of its houses, and to seek the hills. Darkness, emaciation and alteration of the whole; the rain and the inundation narrow their shore. **VI.** A gleam of light breaks through the clouds, and slowly passes over the whole abyss. The crowd becomes silent. Some are borne down and trampled amidst the dead. The waves wash down whole ranks. **X.** One swims to a rock at a distance, but falls down disappointed. **XI.** A mother is the last to die, who throws herself into the waters after the corpse of her child.

§ 2. The Nativity of Jesus. XIII. In spite of the example of the Deluge, man does not correct his vices. **XIV.** Justice requires atonement. XV. An invocation of the Sun. **XVII.** The issuing of Gabriel to the world. **XIX.** He reaches Judaea, and addresses his annunciation to Mary. **XX.** God is conceived and born of her. **XXI.** The angels who had attended him appear when flying hack to heaven, as an eastern star, and guide the shepherds and Magi to find out and adore their God. **XXII.** The devils are roused, and begin tempting Man.

§ 3. The Suffering Mediation of God. XXIII. His infancy. His wanderings. His meekness and love towards the apostles, who he knew would desert, deny and betray him. **XXVI.** An address to Judas. **XXVII.** Ecce Homo! His sufferings before his death. **XXVIII.** Mis death, and Nature's horror. His last words. **XXIX.** A contrast between man and woman at the foot of the cross. **XXX.** His burial; guards are placed round his tomb. **XXXI.** A description of the night of his resurrection. **XXXII.** His resurrection.

§ 4. A Vision of the End of Man's Present State. XXXIII. Death rides upon a steed of poisonous vapours over the earth; in his train are Plague, Pestilence, Slaughter, Terror, and Fear. **XXXVI.** The world presents one great scene of slaughter of the human race. One old man yet remains with life, and dies at sight of a dead grandchild. **XXXVII.** A description of the solitude and peace of the world when Man has passed from its surface. **XLI.** Four angels appear, and call the whole race from the repose of the grave and the caves of punishment, and announce to them another state of trial.

§ 5. The Resurrection and Fatal State of Man. XLIII. Man rises from the caves of pain, from the sleep of the grave, although confined beneath the ocean. God again reveals himself to Man. **XLIX.** Encouraged by the last revelation, all mankind become eager for the path of virtue, and, as all are, at the same ment, in their human spoil, being left untempted by any superior power, they succeed in arriving at ity. **LI.** This trial past, they enter heaven and again mingle with their brother Angels. **LII.** God's reward hose who were virtuous even under temptation.

NTO THE SECOND.

TION I.

E DELUGE.

s had pass'd, and the proud sun, unchanged,
o'er the world, with undiminish'd light.
ling the heavens, with youthful ardour ranged,
Alpine bird just springing to its flight.
after day, as, with his life-bestowing power
noved and bless'd night's heavenly lamp, earth's humblest flower.
seem'd, a dread reproach to passing men,
h giant finger, anxiously to show
ir mockery of God to nature's ken.
t she might rise and let her anger flow.

ength, the hour approach'd, when Justice led
punish man, (for he had fill'd his act,)
Mercy plead no more, hut hide her head
mourn; while Vengeance all its terrors slack'd.
children of the Earth now gaily trod the dance,
scoffing laugh'd and mock'd at Heaven's angry glance.
hat is this God, who patient bears our taunts.
insults and our wrongs? Is he so kind
t e'en he seeks to hide within his haunts.
so forgive because he e'en is blind?"

, while security within their hearts
ot, and look'd not for danger or for ill;
geance the solid rocks, e'en cleaving, parts;
waters of the abyss obey her will.
gling, from the inmost depths, forth they come tumbling out,
bling they rush in waves eddying round about.

The lofty heaven's bright firmament seems split.
Opening a dam, and shows a stagnant pool.
Moving, after long years, in angry fit;
Its banks against the breath of God can't rule.

IV.

Now echoed back, by the dread vault that bears
The weight of chaos stamping at its check,
Rise up the shouts of men; their wildering fears
Are now for life, amidst their country's wreck.
Their sleepless eyes seem starting, in their wild amaze
To see an ocean tread the valley's secret maze.
Then, as the crowded mass of some vast town
Steps on the rising ground, with heightening feet,
And on the wide abyss looks trembling down.
From thousands at each step shrieks mingling meet.

V.

Although the sun is risen, it seems as night;
Hardly are seen the faces of mankind;
And they are such, they seem the eyes to blight
Of friends, who by some gleam each other find.
Hunger has alter'd many, terror and despair
And wolf-eyed conscience alter more with racking care.
The rustling rain, that, dropping now no more,
Comes in unbroken lines upon their heads.
Narrows with darkening flood their straighten'd shore,
And soon the stronger on the weaker treads.

VI.

The outmost crowd, space for a time can gain;
For in the midst, some, fainting into death,
Fall and are trampled on, and lose the pain
And anguish waiting on the other's breath.
At length, their shouts are over, silently they bide,
Dismay'd and speechless; with their heads fixt turn'd aside,
Listening to the boisterous ocean's splash.
Trembling they stand. Mothers alone now hold
Another to the breast, daring the crash;
Husbands and lovers their weak arms unfold.

VII.

The putrid heap, beneath the strong man's feet,
With yielding sliding mass, foul traps can spread,
Against the boasting in his life. There meet
In close embrace the living and the dead.
Heaving with strength and rising from the enclasped bride,
Yon giant-limb'd struggles, but crowds can mock his pride;
The crowds above can force a close embrace,
And, sickening, fainting, but yet struggling still,
He sinks, he sinks, and touches the cold face
Of one he loved, but loathes against his will.

VIII.

There is a break upon the far spread cloud,
And men who watch the angry ocean's splash
Raise up their heads. Light, Light breaks thro' its shroud,
And falls upon the world as lightnings flash.
The vaulting clouds roll on; this solitary beam
Like God's long finger moves, and its far-marking gleam
Seems circling every spot, and pointing out
Waves, waves, waves, waters, and white distant foam;
The eyes of millions follow it about;
It shows the abyss, then fades, no more to roam.

IX.

Now the slow breaking waves (as sickle's sweep
Bears down the outmost of the corn's throng'd mass)
Take down whole lines into the green-eyed deep.
And often o'er the rest quick splashing pass.
A vainly darting arm, some moments struggles, long
Battling the ruthless waves, for agony is strong.
A shuddering cry is heard, before the rush
Of some long wave, that curls upon its prey:
But most fall down, as leaves, silent and hush,
Forced down to death by e'en the lightest spray.

X.

One great in strength, confiding in his power,
Plunges at once and seeks another shore;
A high rock beetles o'er the waves, as tower
That rising lofty views the earth's vast floor,

lie swims, he strives, he reaches the hard scraggy rock,
He climbs and falls; the waves beyond his hopes still mock.
A camel thus, upon the Syrian plain,
When whispering hope bears to its ear the sound
Of freshing fount, hastens its pace to gain
The spot, but, cheated, dead falls on the ground.

XI.

The last of all, a phrensied form is seen,
Listening and laughing, as she hears the foam
Gurgling around the rocks she sits between;
She sits amidst the dead, as midst her home.
Her hands seem grasping image of the pleased mind,
She joys caressing what no other there could find.
The sea has pass'd the rocks, and buoyant forms,
Borne on their swelling airs, now float around;
Oft such are seen round fisher's bark, when storms
Have hush'd that hurl'd earth's girding ships to ground.

XII.

And lo! a corpse borne slow into her sight!
The mother rushes, seizes on the child,
Hugs her to wither'd breasts, with wild affright.
And now no longer laughs by cheats beguiled.
But wildly while the green pale form she clasps, she screams
And shrieks, as the long, rushing, sounding white wave gleams,
Bringing her fear, lest, wash'd again for aye,
The corpse fall from her hand into its grave.
It comes, with the fierce wind; she leaps to die
And perish too in the child. snatching wave.

SECTION II.

THE NATIVITY OF JESUS.

XIII.

Man's race, swept from the earth in sight of those
Whom God in pity saved, was not enough
To make the human breast, that evil knows,
Seek the good path, that seems so harsh and rough.
Thorns cutting deep the flesh, stones with sharp edges thrown

On the straight path, are yet as evil beacons shown;
And children, caught by the gay flower's blow,
By the mild breath of zephyrs, that arise
And cause the heart with wantonness to glow.
Too soon the surer road to good despise.

XIV.

God moved by those, who, guardians of the race,
Attempt to steer, upon the stormy sea
Of Man's rude passions, threw upon the space
Of darkening clouds the rainbow's sign of glee.
This shown, Man needs not dread the wide earth-sweeping rage
Of waters breaking loose his anger to assuage.
Yet Justice claims atonement for the wrong;
Though Mercy pleads, she cannot from his breast
Efface the just, and suff'ring must belong
To crimes, that Justice well atoned may rest.

XV.

My tongue, that until now seem'd confident.
And has thus sung the works and wrongs of Heaven,
Now fails. Unless some inspiration sent
From the high power assist, to silence driven.
It may not hope to speak the attributes divine;
For e'en God's love must glow, must burn in every line;
That love, which for his creatures brought to earth
The sovereign of the heavens, that he might show
(The expiation paid in mortal birth)
The mercy that within did ever glow.

XVI.

O thou! who with thy wheels pausing from sound,
That mingling in soft harmony ascends
And eddies, echoed by the planets round
To heaven, where with its brother notes it blends,
O thou! who with a brow of light look'dst from above
And saw'st descending, on the meek-rayed wings of love,
God to a virgin's womb, inspire my lay!
Thou canst wake life in things inanimate.
O waken in my breast, with thy kind ray,
First love, then power such mercies to relate.

XVII.

The golden gates of heaven flew open wide;
Then passes, messenger unto the world,
A power; at once upon the azure tide
On wings, far stretching, like great sails unfurl'd.
He springs; unclosed a moment yet the gates remain'd,
While cherubs, peeping, sight of the earth's joy obtain'd,
And the far-smiling ocean felt a breath
Loaded with odours from the censer's fume,
Play on its waves, as lover, from the wreath
Of virgin mistress, feels the inhaled perfume.

XVIII.

Then creaking on their brazen hinge, they shut,
While the bright messenger reflects a ray
Of gladness on shamed poverty 's foul hut,
As fluttering through the heavens he wends his May.
At length, upon the Libyan desert, footing ground,
He shakes his glorious wings, and shaking throws around
The dew collected midst the smiling skies,
Which rears amidst the lurid parched sands
An Oasis, and water'd palms arise,
A verdant isle amidst the Ocean lands.

XIX.

Thence with one stride he on Judæa trod.
Seeking the humble cabin of the maid,
lie found her modest, thinking of her God,
Amidst the youthful spring's returning shade.
Her eyes, at sound of man, (from such she deem'd the voice,)
Sought the low ground; she fear'd, though call'd but to rejoice
"Hail, Mary! For thy Lord is now with thee
And shadows thee; and thou, midst women blest,
Shalt cause the evil power from man to flee,
Which now forbids his soul in heaven to rest."

XX.

He said; and God within her womb conceived.
Days, months, e'en pass'd; when he by angels borne
Came to the earth, and she, from pain relieved,

Brought forth her Lord, of all his splendour shorn.
His awful brow sublime put on an infant's smile:
Commanding all, it now a mother would beguile.
Within a manger, when the wind blew hard.
And bore its heavy sleet unto the ground.
The Infant babe midst cattle humbly fared,
While haughty man 'gainst cold a palace found.

XXI.

When born, the attendant angels clustering flew,
Order'd to leave him, and await him there,
Where stands an empty throne, from which love drew
Heaven's majesty a mortal's veil to share.
As their light mingling wings sparkled in the sun's ray,
Their mass appear' d a star that trod the Eastern way.
And kings and shepherds, guided by its light.
Rose from their couch to follow the fair sign,
That promised, as the morning star to night.
Unto their souls, a sun of power benign.

XXII.

They found the child, and, falling at his feet,
Adore their God; for, e'en inspired, they know
That more of power than human sight can meet
Belong'd to him, thus veil'd in human show.
But now the demons rise, from their but seeming trance
To see their king descend; they wake, with haughty glance
They scoffing mock his miserable fare.
Whispering, to man their fell intent inspire,
And make him once again their hatred share
'Gainst God, who with his love their breasts would fire.

SECTION III.

THE SUFFERING MEDIATION OF GOD.

XXIII.

As some wild flower, borne from the blossom'd tree,
Plays on its mother's breath of rich perfume
And wanton circles on the wind, though free,
Allured unto its parent stem and bloom;

Until the rough blast come, that wafts it far away,
And brings a stormy end unto its brightening day;
So the fair child, our Saviour, played around
And seem'd to joy a mother's tender care,
Until his mission urged: then from the ground
He was quick torn, his torturings to bear.

XXIV.

An exile wandering from place to place.
The son of God found not a sheltering roof;
The sparrow and the swallow none will chase
From where they dwell; yet God gave no reproof.
But bearing all, the sick, the wounded and the dead
He raised, and dried the tears that man in grief must shed.
Taunts and revilings, dangers and distress,
Desertion from his friends, mockery from foes,
He doom'd himself to bear, and yet could bless
The very heart that with fell malice glows.

XXV.

E'en while he knew that, flying from his sight,
Apostles should desert him in his need.
He strove to soothe, to make their peril light,
And smiled on him who swore that he would bleed
Ere he would leave a sire so mild, so meek, so kind,
Knowing he should deny him thrice before mankiud.
With him who sold him to his bitter fate,
Remorseless, (as the lamb caress'd and fed.
Nurtured by children for a playful mate.
Is to the knife,) he broke and bless'd his bread.

XXVI.

Judas! When Satan enter'd in thy heart,
Choosing thee out as minister below,
To prove himself but second in his part,
What sign was stampt upon thy human brow?
Did murder bask in thine eye, revel on thy lip
E'en visible to sight, or could he passing dip
Into thy heart, where envy reign'd secure,
And traced its deepening lines so legible,
As if no shame a veil could e'er procure
To hide with shade, what was indelible?

XXVII.

See I where he stands, upon his brow flow down
Drops of his blood, and men can laugh at this!
Laugh at that sceptre, at that thorny crown,
Bestow'd at sign of him who gave the kiss!
See where a man clothed in his brief tho' gorgeous show
Stands pointing with a sneer, then strikes a bitter blow.
Hark at that cry! 'Tis Barabbas it calls;
A robber is preferr'd, and mercy 's shown
The thief; while man's bitterness leaping falls
On him, who leaves for them great heaven's throne.

XXVIII.

How can I speak the rest! The rocks spoke out;
They burst, trammels of nature's sleeping soul,
They burst, indignant, and man's bones about
Were strewn, and men's ghosts were cast forth as foul,
Poisoning the earth and ocean's vainly washing wave;
And heaven refused its light, and hiding darkness gave:
The moon shuddering, averting her bright face,
Look'd on the sun, and hid from his pale eye
The dreadful sight. God said with mercied grace,
"They know not what they do;" then sunk to die.

XXIX.

One man was by his side. Three women stood
And wept; they dared before his foes to weep
And show their love. As the wild torrent flood
Oft sweeps away into its whirling deep
The bolder rock, that rears its hardy daring crest.
And, 'gainst its waves struggling, presents its time-worn breast
But oft it meets a lowly plant, that bends
Before its passing weight, then lifts its head
And smiles upon the wave: So woman lends
A pliant form, but man is broke by terror's tread.

XXX.

At length a man is roused, and seeks the ground
On which God died: careful he takes him down,

Bathes with pure balm and swathes his body round,
And then removes the yet adhering crown.
The women help him in his last sad pious care.
And with him all the pain and all the labour share.
Convey'd at length, as if a mortal tomb
Could hold a God, unto a rocky cave,
They who still doubted, placed around the womb
Of earth some guards; they thought his power to brave.

XXXI.

How beauteous the night when he arose!
The glittering ground seem'd vying with the skies;
Tho' with gay stars its fairy brilliance glows,
The world reflects its beams, its splendour vies.
The smooth unrippled ocean seem'd of burnish'd gold,
The woods on every leaf a various gem uphold.
The virgin moon array'd herself in pride:
Passing midst humble handmaids of her show.
She seem'd with stately march slowly to glide,
And view propitious all the earth below.

XXXII.

The 'guards are sleeping, and the tomb is seal'd.
What is that burst of sound that breaks their dream,
Piercing the rocky sides? "What is reveal'd,
Thus borne upon the light's far-shining gleam?
The God arises, wends his far far stretching flight,
And passes up to heaven on clouds of vapour'd light.
Smiling, his lips seem blessing the low earth,
His hands outstretch'd, held o'er the hurried field.
Seem bidding Mercy waken to new mirth;
Now she may rise, and man from justice shield.

SECTION IV.

A VISION OF THE END OF MAN'S PRESENT STATE.

XXXIII.

A breath, a desolating breath descends;
Death rides upon its power, and ghastly slays
With look of eyeless head; to earth it sends

The foundling birth, the race of other days.
See where his steed, of red and burning vapours got,
Seems the Simoon, slow passing o'er some luckless spot;
When Nature, sweltering in the burning glow.
Calls Zephyrs forth to fan its heated breast,
Such comes from mouth of some deceiving foe.
And blasts the fool that gains its own behest.

XXXIV.

Terror, with shrieks, and fire that gleams on high,
Strikes at the heart, and throws the warrior down.
Fear skulking comes, and with its wandering eye
Seeks whom to touch with holt of ice, unshown.
Pale Pestilence and Plague, and Slaughter's reddening arm
Join in the horrid train, and call on wild Alarm.
She shouts their dreadful names, and speaks their power
To trembling nations prostrate at their feet;
While they with poisons and with daggers lower,
And glut their lust with all the prey they meet.

XXXV.

Their track is mark'd by livid forms, that lay
Putrid and green upon the unmoved sward;
Wolves hungry come, and, scenting at their prey,
Sickening, turn off, and slum their toil's award.
One solitary form rears up its whiten'd crest,
And lifts aside the corpses weighing on its breast:
They are his sons, his daughters, that would shield
Him from the power of death. He ghastly gazes
With his deep sunken eye upon the field,
Then falls upon the child his weak arm raises.

XXXVI.

That lovely child, smiling yet seem'd to live;
It was his daughter's boy, and on her lip
With smiling lips was feeding, and did give
Mirth to her heart; when Slaughter sought to slip
Its weapon in their breasts, and came and pierced both;
But left within their eye the gleam, as, seeming loth
To spoil such beauty, it would leave their joy
Yet decking their young faces brightening glow,
And let him lay a smiling round-cheek'd boy

To kill the sire by such heart-breaking show.

XXXVII.

The cheering song of cottagers' loud glee.
As treading o'er the hill's straight path they bound
To gather grapes from off the bent down tree.
Wakens no more the mountain's softer sound.
No longer now the Zephyrs to the peasant bear
The hum of towns and cities breaking the dark air.
The hammer and the anvil, and the drone,
Slow, pauseless, of the mill, are silent now.
The very sick, have ended e'en their groan;
No more by nature's heard a human throe.

XXXVIII.

Impatient man, who with his grating car
And foaming steeds made the great earth to quake,
Now sleeps; a long-enduring sleep's embrace
Enfolds him now, and nature rest may take.
Alone the avalanches' crash, the torrent's rush
Are heard thro' her vast silent reign, all else is hush.
Even the beasts, who with their loud long bay
Affright the peasant in his bed, are still;
Their face upon the earth dismay'd they lay;
They fear than even man, some greater ill.

XXXIX.

The cities then look'd desolate and lone;
The cottage falls; the wide long palaced street
Was damp, and the rife grass pierced the stone
Untrod, unbroken by the toiling feet.
The hustling ships lay rotting on the rocking wave;
Their strong vast hulks were crumbling, tho' the storms they brave.
The quays, rear'd by the ever-labouring hand.
Sink when man's spirit lied, as did his form;
These worn by the slow spray's consuming band,
This 'neath the weaker lip of biting worm.

XL.

Man's race has pass'd some ages from the earth,

No signs of his long reign are seen below,
But the few whitening bones, that mark the birth
Of some lost form, that pass'd on time's lost flow.
The world seem'd not to grieve; for e'en its widow'd vest
Was gay, and bright in show the colours that it drest.
Upon famed Rome's smooth hills and grassy dells,
London's long plain and Paris' basin'd vale,
The wolf snatch'd the meek lamb; its hunger fell
Now caught no shepherd's threat upon the gale.

XLI.

When, suddenly, on the four points appear
Four angels; their blue vests, floating afar,
Shame e'en the sky once proud its hue to wear,
Holding the winds, they rest upon some star.
Their anxious eyes are fixt, and seem to wait command;
'Tis given: their voice is borne upon the wind's wift band,
"Arise! arise, ye favour'd sons of God!
And leave the scorching caves of burning pain.
Arise, and tread once more where once ye trod,
And seek the seats of lasting bliss to gain.

XLII.

No more your brothers, now, shall tempt your will;
But all, at once, confined in mortal spoil,
You are now call'd your destiny to fill,
And gain your former seats by well-borne toil.
To us 'tis given, to show the mercies of our Lord,
And now, uncheckt by foes, to you our help afford.
Then rise, tho' buried in the moaning deep;
Then rise, tho' sepulchred beneath the mass
Of falling mount! Arise! and rise to weep
Your crimes, and then to bliss eternal pass."

XLIII.

What is that rustling sound, that wakes the ear,
As if a greater vegetation crept
Thro' the mass'd earth, and eager sought to chear
Itself with light and into breathing leapt?
See! the earth, raised, brings forth, and human forms arise,
More numerous than all you wonders of the skies.
See! where yon crowd, following yon dread burst

Of fire and smoke, breaking the solid rock.
Hasten, as if they fled some foe accurst.
And thought its speed would at their hastening mock.

XLIV.

While these, rising, as if from tranquil beds,
Look round, serene, wakening from soundest sleep,
Not e'en disturb'd by dreams, they raise their heads
And smile upon the rest they found so deep.
They recognise the sun; and if a fear is known.
They dread that this is life, which thus again is shown.
Each trembling form, that comes from the deep caves
Where punishment awaits the guilty soul.
Runs to the mountain's brow, and suppliant craves
Its mercied fall to hide their sins so foul.

XLV.

Some to the ocean sands rush in great haste:
But there they meet with crowds shaking the drops
From their thin bodies; and the shore is paced
By thousands, whom not e'en the ocean stops.
But where the bones beneath the waves' light foam did bleach,
The forms as from a winding-sheet stepp'd on the beach.
With the blue waves, their blood is mingled now".
In vain, the coral depths give forth their dead.
O'er their white bones no more the waves may flow.
For e'en the power of death for ever's fled.

XLVI.

The leaves of life, fall'n from the human tree,
(As autumn leaves are raised from the low ground,
And again sudden on the wind seem free
With life to move upon the air around,)
Now rose at once, and their spread dust was animate.
One breath of will, from Him who rules their several state.
Raised them, altho' the trees' autumnal spoil
Numbers not crowds like theirs, when the north wind
With its cold nipping breath and quick-sped toil
Strips off the whole, and leaves no speck behind.

XLVII.

When all were risen, the God reveal'd again
Shone out on man, not in that lowly vest.
Which, suffering, bore the punishment and pain
Due unto us, but in his splendour drest.
To paint the ministering crowds, the thousand bending knees,
The brow, the look sublime, the fair regalities.
Of this last act, 'tis passing my weak tongue.
The power and courts of kings in words may glow
More beautiful; but who has ever sung
In fitting words such scenes, such heavenly show?

XKVIII.

I cannot speak them. All that I can tell
Is, that I seem'd to feel, with millions there,
As if the sight of such a smile could, well,
Win even worse than man from evil's lair.
Still e'en th' alarm of those, who dreaded lest the whole
Of their past torments visit once again their soul,
Cause those, who knew the bliss of the grave's rest,
Look back upon its bed without a sigh;
For such the love that enter'd to the breast,
That all again would to their penance fly.

XLIX.

Jehovah from the sight of man withdrew,
And they were left upon the joyful earth.
But not their life like ours; they evil knew,
But 'twas a dream of wrong before this birth.
Conscious of virtue, now that they had sinn'd was known
By all, and all in penance hoped their grief be shown.
There were no rich, no poor, no suffering rank;
But all bound in one link one father own'd.
And him alone, whom they for mercies thank.
And whom they know on mercy's seat's enthroned.

L.

Putting their thoughts, their words, beneath controul,
They, guided by their guardian angel's rule,
Soon gain command o'er their rebellious soul,
And now no more prove folly's laught at tool.
Long was their trial, long: but they for strength'ning pray'd.

To Power itself, and Power their soul in strength array'd.
They chear'd each other; and the mother's care
Was not to feed her child, but to direct
Its steps in virtue's tracks, with it to share
The penance, and each weakness to correct.

LI.

This trial pass'd, and God open'd the gate
Of starry heaven, and he wing'd the feet
Of all below; for all had fill'd their fate.
And once again the brother angels meet.
These first, lockt in their brothers' arms, their time's employ
And cares, so long bestow'd in vain, recount in joy.
The others then in humble words confess
Their human wrongs, and all at last rejoice.
And turn to their great Sire in thankfulness.
Who answers thus in mildly sounding voice:

LII.

"My children, you on earth have even known
The love, that fathers to their offspring bear:
Their love is but a type of that I 've shown
To those, who have for ages been my care.
But justice yet ordains that I above should show
Reward to those who proved, in trial, virtue's glow.
To these I give the power of sharing all
The bliss they gain, with those who fail'd on earth;
Or, if they will deny this kinder call,
Of leaving those within their later birth.

www.ingramcontent.com/pod-product-compliance
Lightning Source LLC
LaVergne TN
LVHW050612100826
845148LV00015B/3229

9781839675676